Group's

BIBLE SENSE™

1 JOHN

//LIVING IN THE LIGHT OF JESUS

Group

Loveland, Colorado

www.group.com

Group resources actually work!

This Group resource incorporates our R.E.A.L. approach to ministry. It reinforces a growing friendship with Jesus, encourages long-term learning, and results in life transformation, because it's

Relational
Leaner-to-learner interaction enhances learning and builds Christian friendships.

Experiential
What learners experience through discussion and action sticks with them up to 9 times longer than what they simply hear or read.

Applicable
The aim of Chistian education is to equip learners to be both hearers and doers of God's Word.

Learner-based
Learners understand and retain more when the learning process takes into consideration how they learn best.

Group's BIBLESENSE™

1 JOHN: Living in the Light of Jesus
Copyright © 2006 Group Publishing, Inc.

Visit our Web site: **www.group.com**

Credits
Contributors: Kate S. Holburn, Keith Madsen, David Trujillo, and Kelli B. Trujillo
Editor: Carl Simmons
Creative Development Editor: Matt Lockhart
Chief Creative Officer: Joani Schultz
Assistant Editor: Amber Van Schooneveld
Senior Designer: Kari K. Monson
Cover Art Director: Jeff A. Storm
Cover Designer: Andrea Filer
Photographer: Rodney Stewart
Production Manager: DeAnne Lear

Unless otherwise indicated, all Scripture quotations are taken from the *Holy Bible,* New Living Translation, copyright © 1996, 2004. Used by permission of Tyndale House Publishers, Inc., Wheaton, Illinois 60189. All rights reserved.

Library of Congress Cataloging-in-Publication Data
1 John : living in the light of Jesus.-- 1st American pbk. ed.
     p. cm. -- (Group's BibleSense)
  Includes bibliographical references.
  ISBN-13: 978-0-7644-3243-9 (pbk. : alk. paper)
  1. Bible. N.T. Epistle of John, 1st--Study and teaching. 2. Bible. N.T. Epistle of John, 1st--Criticism, interpretation, etc. I. Title: First John. II. Group Publishing. III. Series.
  BS2805.55.A12 2006
  227'.950071--dc22
                              2006008359

ISBN 0-7644-3243-5

10 9 8 7 6 5 4 3 2 1   15 14 13 12 11 10 09 08 07 06
Printed in the United States of America.

CONTENTS

INTRODUCTION TO GROUP'S BIBLESENSE™ 5

ABOUT THE SESSIONS 6

SESSION 1:
LETTING IN THE LIGHT 8
1 John 1:1-10

SESSION 2:
LOVING OTHERS AS JESUS DOES 18
1 John 2:1-17

SESSION 3:
HOLDING ON TO THE TRUTH 30
1 John 2:18-29

SESSION 4:
SHARING THE GIFT OF JESUS' LOVE 40
1 John 3:1-24

SESSION 5:
SHINING OUR LIGHT BRIGHTLY 52
1 John 4:1-21

SESSION 6:
CHOOSING LIFE IN JESUS 62
1 John 5:1-21

LEADER NOTES 75

GROUP ROLES 85

INTRODUCTION

TO GROUP'S BIBLESENSE™

Welcome to **Group's BibleSense**™, a book-of-the-Bible series unlike any you've ever seen! This is a Bible study series in which you'll literally be able to *See, Hear, Smell, Taste, and Touch God's Word*—not only through seeing and hearing the actual book of the Bible you're studying on DVD but also through thought-provoking questions and group activities. As you do these sessions, you'll bring the Word to life, bring your group closer together as a community, and help your group members bring that life to others.

Whether you're new to small groups or have been doing them for years, you'll discover new, exciting, and—dare we say it—*fun* ways to learn and apply God's Word to your life in these sessions. And as you dig deeper into the Bible passage for each session and its meaning to your life, you'll find your life (and the lives around you) transformed more and more into Jesus' likeness.

Each session concludes with a series of opportunities on how to commit to reaching your world with the Bible passage you've just studied—whether it's in changing your own responses to others, reaching out to them individually or as an entire group, or by taking part in something bigger than your group.

So again, welcome to the world of BibleSense! We hope you'll find the experiences and studies here both meaningful and memorable and that as you do them together, your lives will grow even more into the likeness of our Lord, Jesus Christ.

—*Carl Simmons, Editor*

ABOUT THE SESSIONS

TASTE AND SEE (20 minutes)

Every BibleSense session begins with food—to give group members a chance to unwind and transition from a busy day and other preoccupations into the theme of the session. After the food and a few introductory questions, the group gets to experience Scripture in a fresh way. The passage for each session is included on DVD, as well as in print within the book. Also provided is "A Sense of History," a brief feature offering additional cultural and historical context.

DIGGING INTO SCRIPTURE (30 minutes)

This is the central part of the session. The group will have the chance to interact with the Scripture passage you've just read and watched, and, through questions and other sensory experiences, you'll learn how it applies to *your* life.

MAKING IT PERSONAL (15 minutes)

Now you'll move from understanding *how* the passage applies to your life to thinking about ways you *can* apply it. In this part of the session, personal meaning is brought home through meaningful experiences and questions.

TOUCHING YOUR WORLD (25 minutes)

This is the "take home" part of the session. Each group member will choose a weekly challenge to directly apply this session's passage in a practical way in the week ahead, as well as share prayer requests and pray for one another. Also included is a "Taking It Home" section, with tips on how you can prepare for your next session.

GETTING CONNECTED

Pass your books around the room, and have group members write in their names, phone numbers, e-mail addresses, and birthdays.

Name	Phone	E-mail	Birthday

SESSION 1:

LETTING IN THE LIGHT

1 JOHN 1:1-10

In this session you'll see the importance of living in the light of Jesus and learn how to encourage others to do the same.

PRE-SESSION CHECKLIST:

☐ **Leader:** Check out the Session 1 Leader Notes in the back of the book (page 77).

☐ **Food Coordinator:** If you are responsible for the Session 1 snack, see page 88.

☐ **Supplies:**

- 1 lighted makeup mirror for each subgroup

TASTE AND SEE (20 minutes)

"Break bread" with one another. Go ahead—take a piece of the bread that has been prepared.

Did you know? *Bread is called "the staff of life" because it is a primary food source for much of the world's population. In ancient Rome it was considered more vital than meat, and the distribution of grain was central to the welfare system. No wonder Jesus has his disciples pray for their "daily bread" (Matthew 6:11, New International Version) and calls himself "the bread of life" (John 6:35)!*

While enjoying your bread, find a partner—someone you don't know very well—and take a few minutes to discuss the following questions:

- What's one thing you wanted to be when you grew up?

- What's one goal or dream you have for the future?

Gather back together as a large group. Take turns introducing your partner to the group by sharing one thing you learned about him or her that you didn't already know. Choose one of the following questions to answer and share with the group:

- What do you enjoy most about the smell of fresh bread? How does it help you enjoy eating it?

- What memories of freshly baked bread do you have from your childhood? What occasions do you associate with it?

 Watch the first chapter on the DVD (1 John 1:1-10). This passage can also be found on the following pages if you would like to follow along in your book.

1 John 1:1-10

[1]We proclaim to you the one who existed from the beginning, whom we have heard and seen. We saw him with our own eyes and touched him with our own hands. He is the Word of life. [2]This one who is life itself was revealed to us, and we have seen him. And now we testify and proclaim to you that he is the one who is eternal life. He was with the Father, and then he was revealed to us. [3]We proclaim to you what we ourselves have actually seen and heard so that you may have fellowship with us. And our fellowship is with the Father and with his Son, Jesus Christ. [4]We are writing these things so that you may fully share our joy.

[5]This is the message we heard from Jesus and now declare to you: God is light, and there is no darkness in him at all. [6]So we are lying if we say we have fellowship with God but go on living in spiritual darkness; we are not practicing the truth. [7]But if we are living in the light, as God is in the light, then we have fellowship with each other, and the blood of Jesus, his Son, cleanses us from all sin.

[8]If we claim we have no sin, we are only fooling ourselves and not living in the truth. [9]But if we confess our sins to him, he is faithful and just to forgive us our sins and to cleanse us from all wickedness. [10]If we claim we have not sinned, we are calling God a liar and showing that his word has no place in our hearts.

DIGGING INTO SCRIPTURE (30 minutes)

Tip: To maximize participation and also have enough time to work through the session, we recommend breaking into smaller subgroups of three or four at various points during the session.

As a group, discuss:

• What thoughts or emotions came to your mind while watching this session's Bible passage?

Now break into subgroups.

Subgroup Leaders: Find a place where your subgroup can talk with few distractions. Plan to come back together in 15 minutes.

In your subgroup, read 1 John 1:1-10. Pause for two or three seconds at the end of each verse. Close your eyes, and during each pause think about each verse. As a sensory word is used *(heard, seen, touched)*, imagine what those who first read this letter were sensing.

After listening to the passage, read the following "A Sense of History" feature, and answer the questions that follow.

A SENSE OF HISTORY

A Patriarch of the Faith

John, "the disciple Jesus loved" (John 21:20, 24), is the author of this book. By the time John wrote this letter, he was a patriarch of the Christian faith; tradition suggests he lived into his nineties.

When we read of John in the Gospels, he is a young man—throwing out and pulling in heavy fishing nets, hiking around the country with Jesus. He and his brother James were called "Sons of Thunder" (Mark 3:17) by Jesus. We don't know for sure what Jesus meant by that nickname, but it seems to speak of men who were both vigorous and possibly harsh. In one incident they were prepared to have a Samaritan village destroyed for not giving them hospitality on their way to Jerusalem (Luke 9:54); they also irritated the other disciples by trying to get special considerations from Jesus (Mark 10:35-41).

What changed John from an apparently self-focused young man to the old patriarch who repeatedly called Christians to love one another? Most certainly it was his experience with Jesus. Is it coincidental that someone who called himself "the disciple Jesus loved" was able to say so much about loving others, as John does in this letter?

- When have you been an eyewitness to a "big" event? How did it affect the way you saw and talked about that event?

- Why is it important for us to know that John and the other disciples heard and saw and touched Jesus?

- When is a time you were able to share your own experience with Jesus with others? What was the result?

Come back together as a larger group, and share any highlights or questions from your subgroup discussion.

Break back into subgroups.

Leader: Give each subgroup a makeup mirror. Make sure the mirrors are lit first; then turn off all the other lights in the room.

Sit in front of the mirror, one at a time. Say a few words aloud about what the light reveals about your face—both what you like and what you *don't* like. The one looking in the mirror is the only one who should comment.

After everyone has taken a turn, answer the following:

• How is looking into the light of the mirror like or unlike how people react when they first encounter the light of Jesus?

Reread 1 John 1:5-10, and answer the following questions:

• How can confessing our sins and flaws to each other help us have fellowship with one another? with Jesus?

> "*It is better to light a candle than to curse the darkness.*"
> —Old Chinese Proverb

Leave the makeup mirrors on, and come back together as a larger group and share any highlights or questions from your subgroup discussion.

MAKING IT PERSONAL (15 minutes)

Leader: Turn off the makeup mirrors in the room.

In the dark, answer the following questions:

• What was the "darkest" time of your life? Why was it so dark?

• What are some ways you've encountered *spiritual* darkness in your life? What contributed to that darkness? How did you find your way out?

Leader: Turn the lights back on.

Answer the following questions:

• Think about your reaction to the lights coming back on. Why might some people prefer living in darkness to coming into Jesus' light?

• What's one thing you can do to help bring someone avoiding the light of Jesus out of his or her darkness?

> *Did you know? Eyes adjust between dark and light by changing the size of the pupil and through the action of light-sensitive cells in the retina called rods and cones. Rods only receive shades of gray and function best in dim light. Cones distinguish color and function best in bright light. Therefore, when our world becomes darker, it also becomes a less colorful place.*

TOUCHING YOUR WORLD (25 minutes)

Review the following "weekly challenge" options, and select the challenge you'd like to do. Turn to a partner, and share your choice. Then make plans to connect with your partner sometime between now and the next session to check in and encourage one another.

☐ **STUDY YOUR BIBLE EACH DAY.** Make a special effort this week to study the Bible daily and to find a specific application to your life from the passage you're studying. Let the light of God's Word illuminate your life and show you where change needs to happen. Each day, write down your answers to these two questions: "What does this passage say?" and "How do I need to change because of what I have read?"

☐ **GET RID OF THE DARKNESS IN YOUR LIFE.** Perhaps you have a relationship where hate and bitterness hold sway. Bring the light of forgiveness into it. Perhaps you have let dishonesty creep into your business. Let in the light of Christian integrity. Find another Christian to confess to and hold you accountable. While it is true that we can confess our sins directly to God, there is great value in confessing to another person as well. It forces us to be honest with ourselves and take our sins seriously, and it also helps us experience God's forgiveness more personally. Choose someone you trust to maintain confidentiality.

☐ **SHARE THE LIGHT OF JESUS CHRIST.** Make a point to tell at least one other person one way in which your relationship with Jesus has made a difference in your life. Remember that when light first comes to someone in darkness, it can be uncomfortable and may meet with resistance. Don't be pushy—simply be open about how the light of Jesus has changed your own life.

Come back together as a group. Share prayer requests.

Dim the lights once more to set the mood—and as a reminder that Jesus is our light in whatever darkness we're praying against.

Before the leader prays, take a few moments to be silent and appreciate God's goodness in your life.

Leader: If you haven't already, take a few minutes to review the group roles and assignments (page 85) with the group. At minimum, be sure the food and supplies responsibilities for the next session are covered.

Until next time...

Date _____

Time _____

Place _____

Taking It Home:

1. Set a goal for how many times you'll either read through or watch on your DVD the Session 2 Bible passage (1 John 2:1-17). Make a point to read the "A Sense of History" feature in Session 2 (page 22) prior to the next session. You may also want to review this week's passage. Let your weekly challenge partner know what goals you've set, so he or she can encourage you and help hold you accountable.

2. Touch base sometime before the next session with your weekly challenge partner to compare notes on how you're both doing with the goals you've set.

3. If you have volunteered for a role or signed up to help with food or supplies for the next session, be sure to prepare for this. The Session 2 Supplies list can be found on page 18, and the Food Coordinator instructions are on page 88.

4. **I commit to touching my world this week by living in Jesus' light in the following ways:**

_____

_____

_____

SESSION 2:

LOVING OTHERS AS JESUS DOES

1 JOHN 2:1-17

In this session you'll learn more about how we can love one another just as Jesus loves *us*.

PRE-SESSION CHECKLIST:

☐ **Leader:** Check out the Session 2 Leader Notes in the back of the book (page 79).

☐ **Food Coordinator:** If you are responsible for the Session 2 snack, see page 88.

☐ **Supplies:**
- 1 extra chair

TASTE AND SEE | (20 minutes)

This session begins with a childhood snack—milk and cookies! (Sorry, no naps afterward.)

> "*These are the things I learned…Warm cookies and cold milk are good for you.*"
>
> —Robert Fulghum, All I Really Need to Know I Learned in Kindergarten

While eating, discuss the following questions:

• What foods do you associate with your childhood?

• What memories do you associate with those foods?

• In what ways do you feel like a child even now? Is that a good thing or a bad thing? Why?

 Watch the second chapter on the DVD (1 John 2:1-17). This passage can also be found on the following pages if you would like to follow along in your book.

1 John 2:1-17

¹My dear children, I am writing this to you so that you will not sin. But if anyone does sin, we have an advocate who pleads our case before the Father. He is Jesus Christ, the one who is truly righteous. ²He himself is the sacrifice that atones for our sins—and not only our sins but the sins of all the world.

³And we can be sure that we know him if we obey his commandments. ⁴If someone claims, "I know God," but doesn't obey God's commandments, that person is a liar and is not living in the truth. ⁵But those who obey God's word truly show how completely they love him. That is how we know we are living in him. ⁶Those who say they live in God should live their lives as Jesus did.

⁷Dear friends, I am not writing a new commandment for you; rather it is an old one you have had from the very beginning. This old commandment—to love one another—is the same message you heard before. ⁸Yet it is also new. Jesus lived the truth of this commandment, and you also are living it. For the darkness is disappearing, and the true light is already shining.

⁹If anyone claims, "I am living in the light," but hates a Christian brother or sister, that person is still living in darkness. ¹⁰Anyone who loves another brother or sister is living in the light and does not cause others to stumble. ¹¹But anyone who hates another brother or sister is still living and walking in darkness. Such a person does not know the way to go, having been blinded by the darkness.

¹²I am writing to you who are God's children

because your sins have been forgiven through Jesus.

¹³I am writing to you who are mature in the faith

because you know Christ, who existed from the beginning.

I am writing to you who are young in the faith

because you have won your battle with the evil one.

¹⁴I have written to you who are God's children

because you know the Father.

I have written to you who are mature in the faith

because you know Christ, who existed from the beginning.

I have written to you who are young in the faith

because you are strong.

God's word lives in your hearts,

and you have won your battle with the evil one.

¹⁵Do not love this world nor the things it offers you, for when you love the world, you do not have the love of the Father in you. ¹⁶For the world offers only a craving for physical pleasure, a craving for everything we see, and pride in our achievements and possessions. These are not from the Father, but are from this world. ¹⁷And this world is fading away, along with everything that people crave. But anyone who does what pleases God will live forever.

A SENSE OF HISTORY

Light and Darkness in John's Time

Images of light and darkness, used by John more than any other New Testament writer, were popular during the first century, and not just among Christians.

The Essene sect of Judaism, which separated from the rest of Israel and settled near the Dead Sea, had among its writings a scroll called *War of the Sons of Light against the Sons of Darkness* (the Essenes being the "sons of light").

The Gnostics, a mystical group who thought they alone had "true knowledge" of the nature of reality and salvation, also saw the world as being in a duel between light and darkness—and saw followers of Christ on the side of darkness.

In contrast, John presents Jesus as the true light, using imagery of light and darkness more than any other New Testament writer. While doing so, John echoes the words of the Old Testament prophet Isaiah, written hundreds of years earlier. In the book of Isaiah, God calls Israel to "let [their] light shine for all to see" (Isaiah 60:1-3). God promises great success if they are obedient to that calling: "Feed the hungry, and help those in trouble. Then your light will shine out from the darkness, and the darkness around you shall be as bright as noon" (Isaiah 58:10).

Thus, in this letter, John deliberately reclaims the power of Old Testament imagery from those who were misusing it and turns it back toward "the light of the world"—Jesus (John 9:5).

DIGGING INTO SCRIPTURE (30 minutes)

As a group, discuss:

• What thoughts or emotions came to your mind while watching this session's Bible passage, whether just now or during the past week?

Now break into subgroups.

Subgroup Leaders: Find a place where your subgroup can talk with few distractions. Plan to come back together in 10 minutes.

Read 1 John 2:1-8 in your subgroups, and answer the following questions:

• What's your reaction to John's challenge to live our lives as Jesus did? Does that challenge inspire you? intimidate you? provoke some other response?

> "Do not seek revenge or bear a grudge against one of your people, but love your neighbor as yourself."
>
> —Leviticus 19:18, NIV

• Read Leviticus 19:18, in the margin. How is this commandment both old and new? How does knowing that this was also an Old Testament command affect your response to John's challenge?

Come back together as a larger group, and share any highlights or questions from your subgroup discussion.

Break back into subgroups. Family members or couples should be in separate subgroups for this activity.

Each person will make up three statements about himself or herself. Two of the statements should be truths that the subgroup wouldn't know and which are not easily verified ("I shoplifted in the sixth grade," *not* "I have blue eyes."). The third statement should be false. People will take turns sharing their three "truths"; the rest of the group will vote on which statement they think is the false one.

After everyone's had a turn, answer the following questions:

• How easy or difficult was it to make up a false statement about yourself? How well were you able to hide the truth from the rest of the subgroup?

• What clues helped you figure out when others weren't telling the truth?

- Look again at 1 John 2:3-6. What does John say is the surest sign that someone is lying about his or her love for God?

- What's one way you've failed to love others as Jesus did? What's one thing you can do to change that?

> "*Almost all lies are acts, and speech has no part in them.*"
> —Mark Twain,
> "My First Lie, and How I Got Out of It"

Come back together as a larger group, and share any highlights or questions from your subgroup discussion.

MAKING IT PERSONAL (15 minutes)

Read 1 John 2:7-11.

Leader: Put the extra chair in the middle of your group.

The person with the earliest birthday in the year should sit in the chair first. Focusing on the person in the chair, everyone else should complete the following sentence: "You have brought light to this group by..."

Continuing in order of birthday, have each person in your group sit in the chair and receive affirmation from the rest of the group. After everyone has had a turn, answer the following questions:

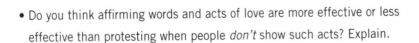

- How did it feel to receive these affirmations? to give them?

- Do you think affirming words and acts of love are more effective or less effective than protesting when people *don't* show such acts? Explain.

- What's one thing you can do, in your home or outside of it, to encourage expressions of love and better meet the challenge of loving others as Jesus did?

TOUCHING YOUR WORLD (25 minutes)

Review the following weekly challenge options, and select the challenge you'd like to do. Turn to a partner, and share your choice. Then make plans to connect with your partner sometime between now and the next session to check in and encourage one another.

☐ **MAKE PEACE WITH ANOTHER PERSON.** Is there another person you've been at odds with? Commit to seek him or her out and set things right this week. This could be anything from offering to talk over your differences, to sending that person a card indicating that you are praying for him or her, to sharing words of affirmation with him or her.

☐ **DEVELOP A HABIT OF AFFIRMING OTHERS.** Make a goal of affirming a certain number of people during each day this week (but feel free to go above and beyond!). Keep a journal so you can write down how these affirmations appear to affect the people to whom you give them.

☐ **VOLUNTEER FOR AN OUTREACH MINISTRY.** Show Christ's love in a concrete way by committing to a hands-on ministry this week. It could be feeding the hungry or visiting the sick or shut-in. Or maybe someone needs a home repair or car repair that you can help provide for financially (or maybe even do yourself or with a group). Think about how showing this love to others has affected how you feel about yourself and people in general.

Come back together as a group. Share prayer requests, and then pray for everyone's needs. Pray also that God would give you a deeper appreciation of each person in the group.

Until next time...

Date _____

Time _____

Place _____

Taking It Home:

1. Set a goal for how many times you'll either read through or watch on your DVD the Session 3 Bible passage (1 John 2:18-29). Make a point to read the "A Sense of History" feature in Session 3 (page 33) before the next session. You may also want to review this week's passage—or even watch the entire book of 1 John straight through. (It takes about 17 minutes.) Let your weekly challenge partner know what goals you've set, so he or she can encourage you and help hold you accountable.

2. Touch base sometime before the next session with your weekly challenge partner to compare notes on how you're both doing with the goals you've set.

3. If you have volunteered for a role or signed up to help with food or supplies for the next session, be sure to prepare for this. The Session 3 Supplies list can be found on page 30, and the Food Coordinator instructions are on page 88.

4. **I commit to touching my world this week by loving others as Jesus would in the following ways:**

_____

_____

_____

_____

HOLDING ON TO THE TRUTH

1 JOHN 2:18-29

In this session you'll discover what we can do to hold on to and live out the truth Jesus gives us.

PRE-SESSION CHECKLIST:

☐ **Leader:** Check out the Session 3 Leader Notes in the back of the book (page 81).

☐ **Food Coordinator:** If you are responsible for the Session 3 snack, see page 88.

☐ **Supplies:**

- 1 blindfold for every 2 people in the group

- Assortment of everyday objects such as a cell phone, magazine, CD case, empty soda can, candle, tissue box, or credit card—one object for every two people in the group

- Sticky notes—at least 3 per person

- 1 pen or pencil for everyone in the group

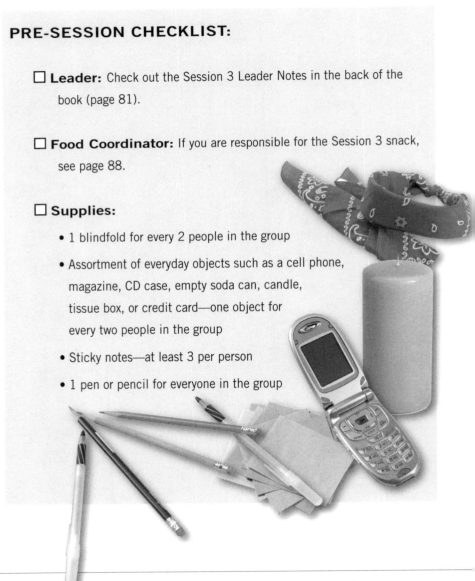

TASTE AND SEE (20 minutes)

Enjoy this session's food.

Set up at least one of your crackers in the following manner (even if you don't eat it): Put spread on the cracker and a piece of meat on top of the spread. Save that cracker for your discussion (but go ahead and enjoy the others!).

Hold up the cracker you made. Flip it over, holding on to just the cracker part (but keep your plate or hand underneath, just in case!). Then discuss the following questions:

- What function does the spread perform? Why is that important?

- Think of this snack as representing your relationship with God. When have you felt "stuck to," or close to, God—even when your world seemed upside-down? What was that like?

Now pull the meat off the cracker, and hold the meat in one hand and the cracker in the other.

- When have you felt pulled away from God like this? What was *that* like?

Watch the Session 3 chapter on the DVD (1 John 2:18-29). This passage can also be found on the following pages.

1 John 2:18-29

18Dear children, the last hour is here. You have heard that the Antichrist is coming, and already many such antichrists have appeared. From this we know that the last hour has come. 19These people left our churches, but they never really belonged with us; otherwise they would have stayed with us. When they left, it proved that they did not belong with us.

20But you are not like that, for the Holy One has given you his Spirit, and all of you know the truth. 21So I am writing to you not because you don't know the truth but because you know the difference between truth and lies. 22 And who is a liar? Anyone who says that Jesus is not the Christ. Anyone who denies the Father and the Son is an antichrist. 23Anyone who denies the Son doesn't have the Father, either. But anyone who acknowledges the Son has the Father also.

24So you must remain faithful to what you have been taught from the beginning. If you do, you will remain in fellowship with the Son and with the Father. 25And in this fellowship we enjoy the eternal life he promised us.

26I am writing these things to warn you about those who want to lead you astray. 27But you have received the Holy Spirit, and he lives within you, so you don't need anyone to teach you what is true. For the Spirit teaches you everything you need to know, and what he teaches is true—it is not a lie. So just as he has taught you, remain in fellowship with Christ.

28And now, dear children, remain in fellowship with

Christ so that when he returns, you will be full of courage and not shrink back from him in shame.

[29]Since we know that Christ is righteous, we also know that all who do what is right are God's children.

A SENSE OF HISTORY
False vs. True

After Paul's death, it's likely that John continued Paul's ministry in Asia Minor, encouraging and teaching Christians there. Scholars believe that as an older man John resided in Ephesus, pastoring a church there and witnessing firsthand the growth of the heresy of Gnosticism.

Although different Gnostic sects disagreed on some matters, they shared the belief that they had received a special knowledge (*gnosis*) that could only be passed along through "secret" teachings. The Gnostics also considered matter to be evil—which in turn led to the beliefs that the Old Testament God who created matter was also evil and that Jesus, the God of the New Testament, did not actually appear in the flesh.

One of the leaders of "Christian Gnosticism" in Ephesus was Cerinthus, who no doubt inspired much of the vigorous opposition shown by John in this letter. One account from early church history relates, "the apostle John once entered a bath to bathe; but, when he learned that Cerinthus was within, he sprang from his place and rushed out of the door, for he could not bear to remain under the same roof with him. He advised those who were with him to do the same. 'Let us flee,' he said, 'lest the bath fall, for Cerinthus, the enemy of truth, is within.' "

Since it's likely that John was writing this letter to several Asiatic communities, it's also possible that Colossae—another city farther inland from the coastal Ephesus—was one of the addressees. Several years prior, Paul had urged the Colossians to resist similar false teaching. For more of the story, read Colossians 2:4-23 on your own time.

DIGGING INTO SCRIPTURE (30 minutes)

As a group, discuss:

• What thoughts or emotions came to mind while watching this session's Bible passage, whether just now or during the past week?

At this time, break up into subgroups.

Subgroup Leaders: Find a place where your subgroup can talk with few distractions. Plan to come back together in 15 minutes.

Read 1 John 2:18-23, and answer the following questions:

• What's your reaction to John's statement in verse 19?

• What does John say about those "liars" and "antichrists" who are separated from God?

• What lies or enemies of Jesus do you see in our world today?

Come back together as a larger group, and share any highlights or questions from your subgroup discussion.

 Break into pairs. Blindfold one person in each pair.

Leader: Take those people who are *not* blindfolded to a separate room, and have each person take one of the everyday objects from your Supplies list. Also see your Leader Notes for this session (page 81) for further instructions.

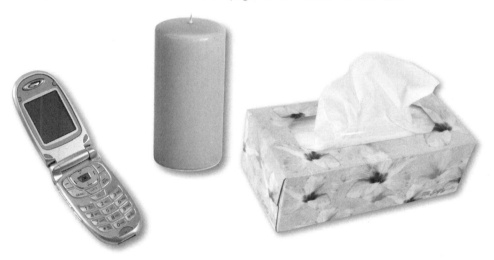

Those who aren't blindfolded should take a minute or so to describe the object they're holding to the blindfolded person. Then hand the object to the blindfolded person, and spend another minute describing it to him or her.

When you're done, let the blindfolded person remove his or her blindfold. Come back together as a group, and answer the following questions:

- What was it like to be blindfolded during this experience? to be the "persuader"?

- How easy or difficult was it to figure out what the object was once you held it?

- What things help us distinguish and hold on to spiritual truths amid the confusion and falsehoods we face each day?

"*O God, who art the Truth, make me one with Thee in everlasting love…in Thee is all that I wish for and desire. Let all the doctors hold their peace; let all creation keep silence before Thee: speak Thou alone to me.*"
—*Thomas à Kempis*

- How do you think God wants us to respond to those who believe something other than God's truth? Give specific examples.

MAKING IT PERSONAL (15 minutes)

Read 1 John 2:24-29.

 **Leader:** Distribute the sticky notes. Make sure everyone has something to write with.

On each sticky note, write down a "God truth" you discovered or were reminded of during this session. Attach each sticky note to yourself, anywhere you'd like.

When everyone's done, answer the following questions:

- Describe a time you struggled to determine what the spiritual truth in a situation was. How did the Holy Spirit guide you through that time?

- How are the sticky notes that are attached to you similar to the way the Spirit shows us God's truth? How are they different?

- How much of a priority is it for you to "remain in fellowship with Christ"? What's one way you can invite the Spirit to help you do that more successfully?

> **Did you know?**
> A 3M researcher named Spencer Silver invented sticky-note adhesive in 1968—unintentionally. He was trying to create a strong adhesive but instead created a weak one.
>
> In 1974, Arthur Fry came up with the idea of using the adhesive on special bookmarks. Where did he have this brainstorm? In church choir—while looking at a hymnal.

TOUCHING YOUR WORLD (25 minutes)

Review the following weekly challenge options, and select the challenge you'd like to do. Turn to a partner, and share your choice. Then make plans to connect with your partner sometime between now and the next session to check in and encourage one another.

☐ **ENJOY FELLOWSHIP WITH GOD.** Set aside at least an hour this week to enjoy fellowship with God in your own unique way: Sing worship songs; go for a hike and enjoy the beauty of nature; create art—any way you'd like to express your praise! Thank God just for being God...for eternal life...that the Holy Spirit lives inside you—and isn't going anywhere...whatever you'd like.

☐ **TUNE IN TO THE SPIRIT DAILY.** Commit to a time each day (such as first thing in the morning or last thing at night) to read Scripture and to reflect quietly on God's Word and on the day ahead (or the day you've just had). Avoid unnecessary distractions—simply listen. As you gain a sense of the Spirit's leading in an area of your life, commit to live it out.

☐ **RECOGNIZE LIES, AND REPLACE THEM WITH GOD'S TRUTH.** Are there any lies you've been struggling against? Ask God to reveal his truth in that situation. Prayerfully keep your ears and eyes open for any other lies you encounter. However, if you run across anyone who's spreading spiritual lies, don't be harsh or condemning. Gently ask if you can discuss the topic, and lovingly share what you think is true and why. Do something to show that person God's grace and love in action. Finally, pray for that person.

Come back together as a group. Share prayer requests, and then pray for everyone's needs. Take time to ask God to reveal any places where you've been struggling against lies in your life and how to shine the light of Jesus' truth into those places.

Until next time...

Date _____

Time _____

Place _____

Taking It Home:

1. Set a goal for how many times you'll either read through or watch on your DVD the Session 4 Bible passage (1 John 3:1-24). Make a point to read the "A Sense of History" feature in Session 4 (page 44) before the next session. You may also want to review this week's passage—or even watch the entire book of 1 John straight through. (It takes about 17 minutes.) Let your weekly challenge partner know what goals you've set, so he or she can encourage you and help hold you accountable.

2. Touch base sometime before the next session with your weekly challenge partner to compare notes on how you're both doing with the goals you've set.

3. If you have volunteered for a role or signed up to help with food or supplies for the next session, be sure to prepare for this. The Session 4 Supplies list can be found on page 40, and the Food Coordinator instructions are on page 89.

4. **I commit to touching my world this week by holding on to Jesus' truth in the following ways:**

_____

_____

_____

_____

SESSION 4:

SHARING THE GIFT OF JESUS' LOVE

1 JOHN 3:1-24

In this session you'll reflect on the gifts God has given us and practical ways to share those gifts with others.

PRE-SESSION CHECKLIST:

☐ **Leader:** Check out the Session 4 Leader Notes in the back of the book (page 82).

☐ **Food Coordinator:** If you are responsible for the Session 4 snack, see page 89.

☐ **Supplies:**
- 6 dominoes per group member

TASTE AND SEE (20 minutes)

Today's snack is bread with jam. Each person should take a turn spreading jam on a piece of bread and then giving it to the person on his or her right.

After everyone has eaten his or her bread, discuss the following questions:

• The jam gave an extra bit of sweetness to the snack we gave each other. What unexpected "sweetness" have you received from others recently? from God?

• What's the most special gift you remember receiving? What made it so special?

 Watch the Session 4 chapter on the DVD (1 John 3:1-24).

1 John 3:1-24

¹See how very much our Father loves us, for he calls us his children, and that is what we are! But the people who belong to this world don't recognize that we are God's children because they don't know him. ²Dear friends, we are already God's children, but he has not yet shown us what we will be like when Christ appears. But we do know that we will be like him, for we will see him as he really is. ³And all who have this eager expectation will keep themselves pure, just as he is pure.

⁴Everyone who sins is breaking God's law, for all sin is contrary to the law of God. ⁵And you know that Jesus came to take away our sins, and there is no sin in him. ⁶Anyone who continues to live in him will not sin. But anyone who keeps on sinning does not know him or understand who he is.

⁷Dear children, don't let anyone deceive you about this: When people do what is right, it shows that they are righteous, even as Christ is righteous. ⁸But when people keep on sinning, it shows that they belong to the devil, who has been sinning since the beginning. But the Son of God came to destroy the works of the devil. ⁹Those who have been born into God's family do not make a practice of sinning, because God's life is in them. So they can't keep on sinning, because they are children of God. ¹⁰So now we can tell who are children of God and who are children of the devil. Anyone who does not live righteously and does not love other believers does not belong to God.

¹¹This is the message you have heard from the beginning: We should love one another. ¹²We must not be like Cain, who belonged to the evil one and killed his brother. And why did he kill him? Because Cain had been doing what was evil, and his brother

had been doing what was righteous. ¹³So don't be surprised, dear brothers and sisters, if the world hates you.

¹⁴If we love our Christian brothers and sisters, it proves that we have passed from death to life. But a person who has no love is still dead. ¹⁵Anyone who hates another brother or sister is really a murderer at heart. And you know that murderers don't have eternal life within them.

¹⁶We know what real love is because Jesus gave up his life for us. So we also ought to give up our lives for our brothers and sisters. ¹⁷If someone has enough money to live well and sees a brother or sister in need but shows no compassion—how can God's love be in that person?

¹⁸Dear children, let's not merely say that we love each other; let us show the truth by our actions. ¹⁹Our actions will show that we belong to the truth, so we will be confident when we stand before God. ²⁰Even if we feel guilty, God is greater than our feelings, and he knows everything.

²¹Dear friends, if we don't feel guilty, we can come to God with bold confidence. ²²And we will receive from him whatever we ask because we obey him and do the things that please him.

²³And this is his commandment: We must believe in the name of his Son, Jesus Christ, and love one another, just as he commanded us. ²⁴Those who obey God's commandments remain in fellowship with him, and he with them. And we know he lives in us because the Spirit he gave us lives in us.

A SENSE OF HISTORY
Seeing God's Love—and Showing It

As one of Jesus' disciples, John was an eyewitness to Jesus' radical acts of love—including his death on the cross (John 19:16-30). Therefore, John learned how to extend the same kind of love to those around him.

One example is found in the Gospel he wrote, at the scene of the Crucifixion: "When Jesus saw his mother standing there beside the disciple he loved, he said to her, 'Dear woman, here is your son.' And he said to this disciple, 'Here is your mother.' And from then on this disciple took her into his home" (John 19:26-27). The love and care John showed Jesus' mother was an active reflection of God's own love.

Church tradition indicates that John later settled in Ephesus and was the only one of the original 12 to die of old age. Jerome, the foremost biblical scholar of the ancient church, reports that when John became too weak to walk, he was carried to church meetings. He adds that on John's deathbed, his disciples asked him if he had any last message to leave them. "Little children," he said, "love one another." When asked if that was all, he responded, "It is enough...for it is the Lord's command."

DIGGING INTO SCRIPTURE (30 minutes)

As a group, discuss:

• What thoughts or emotions came to your mind while watching this session's Bible passage?

Now break into subgroups.

Leader: Give each person in the subgroups six dominoes.

Read 1 John 3:1-17 in your subgroup, and answer the following questions:

• How easy or difficult is it for you to accept the idea that you're God's child? that all Christians will someday be like Jesus?

• In what ways does this "eager expectation" help keep you "pure, just as he is pure"?

• What's your understanding of verses 4-10? Does it mean that everyone who sins doesn't belong to God? Explain your answer.

> **On your own time:**
> For a deeper understanding of 1 John 3:13, read the accounts of Christians who have been hated—persecuted, tortured, or killed. You can read online accounts or books, such as Foxe's Book of Martyrs by John Foxe.

Use all your subgroup's dominoes to set up a sequence in which all the dominoes will fall if the first one is tipped over (but don't tip it over *yet!*). Be creative—make it twist and turn however you like.

Take a maximum of three minutes to set up the sequence. When the setup is complete, answer the following questions:

- What's the connection between the dominoes you've set up? How many dominoes do you think could be removed without affecting that connection?

Extra Impact:

Go ahead and actually remove three to five dominoes from the middle of the sequence. Then, tip over the very first domino, and see how the dominoes fall. Wait until the sequence has fallen up to the missing dominoes, and then continue your subgroup discussion.

- How is this like or unlike being connected with other Christians? Which domino would you be in this sequence? Explain.

Read 1 John 3:18-24 in your subgroups. Then tip over the first domino, and watch as the sequence is completed. Answer the following questions:

- John talks about loving others as Jesus loves us. How does what you just did represent this idea?

- What's one way you can let Jesus' love for you "topple into" your love for others?

Stay in your subgroups for the next part of this session.

> "How many are called physicians, who know not how to heal! how many are called watchers, who sleep all night long! So, many are called Christians, and yet in deeds are not found such; because they are not this which they are called, that is, in life, in manners, in faith, in hope, in charity."
>
> —St. Augustine, "Homilies on the First Epistle of John"

MAKING IT PERSONAL (15 minutes)

Each person in the subgroup should take a single domino.

Reread 1 John 3:16-20, and answer the following questions:

• How does John's command to "give up our lives for our brothers and sisters" make you feel? Challenged? Frightened? Overwhelmed? Something else?

• Regardless of your reaction, why is it still important to make this our goal? How does knowing that Jesus gave up his own life for us help us stay focused on that goal?

• Think of someone you've had a particularly hard time showing Jesus' love to. What's one practical way you could "give up your life" for that person?

Come back together as a larger group, and share any highlights or questions from your subgroup discussion. Take your domino home with you as a reminder to live the truth of God's love.

TOUCHING YOUR WORLD (25 minutes)

Review the following weekly challenge options, and select the challenge you'd like to do. Turn to a partner, and share your choice. Then make plans to connect with your partner sometime between now and the next session to check in and encourage one another.

☐ **"SEE" HOW MUCH GOD LOVES YOU.** This week sit down, and write all the ways you can think of that God shows his love to you. Maybe it's in a quiet moment with God; maybe it's through laughter with your close friends; maybe it's a special Scripture verse that speaks to your heart. As you see examples during the week, write them down, and take time to thank God right then and there for that gift. At the end of the week, read over everything you've written, and thank God some more. Share what you've learned with someone else.

☐ **GET RIGHT WITH GOD.** How have you been disobeying God? Are there specific or habitual sins you've been continuing in? Confess those sins, thank God for his forgiveness, and commit to continue to seek God's help in fully abandoning those sins. Avoid the things that tempt you, and find a trusted Christian friend to hold you accountable.

☐ **GET RIGHT WITH OTHERS.** Have you hurt someone else? Is there hatred or resentment you need to be forgiven of—or forgive others of? Set aside a block of time with that person—over dinner or a cup of coffee—and bring God's forgiveness into that relationship. Commit to replace hate or anger with God's love, and pray regularly that God will change your attitude toward that person. Pray about this now and during the week; then follow through.

☐ **SHARE GOD'S LOVE.** "Give up" your life for someone in a practical way. Find a way to show compassion to someone in need. Fill a gas tank, buy a hot meal, or just provide a listening ear. Commit to do something meaningful that requires your intentional time and effort.

Come back together as a group. Share prayer requests, and then pray for everyone's needs. But don't just focus on needs—be sure also to pray for opportunities for everyone in the group to share Jesus' love this week.

Until next time...

Date _____

Time _____

Place _____

Taking It Home:

1. Set a goal for how many times you'll either read through or watch on your DVD the Session 5 Bible passage (1 John 4:1-21). Make a point to read the "A Sense of History" feature in Session 5 (page 56) before the next session. Let your weekly challenge partner know what goals you've set, so he or she can encourage you and help hold you accountable.

2. Touch base sometime before the next session with your weekly challenge partner to compare notes on how you're both doing with the goals you've set.

3. If you have volunteered for a role or signed up to help with food or supplies for the next session, be sure to prepare for this. The Session 5 Supplies list can be found on page 52, and the Food Coordinator instructions are on page 89.

4. **I commit to touching my world this week by sharing the love of Jesus in the following ways:**

_____

_____

_____

_____

SESSION 5:

SHINING OUR LIGHT BRIGHTLY

1 JOHN 4:1-21

In this session you'll explore how true Christ-followers can stand out to the rest of the world.

PRE-SESSION CHECKLIST:

☐ **Leader:** Check out the Session 5 Leader Notes in the back of the book (page 83).

☐ **Food Coordinator:** If you are responsible for the Session 5 snack, see page 89.

☐ **Supplies:**
- 1 local "Help Wanted" page for each subgroup
- 1 pen for each subgroup
- 1 piece of paper for each subgroup

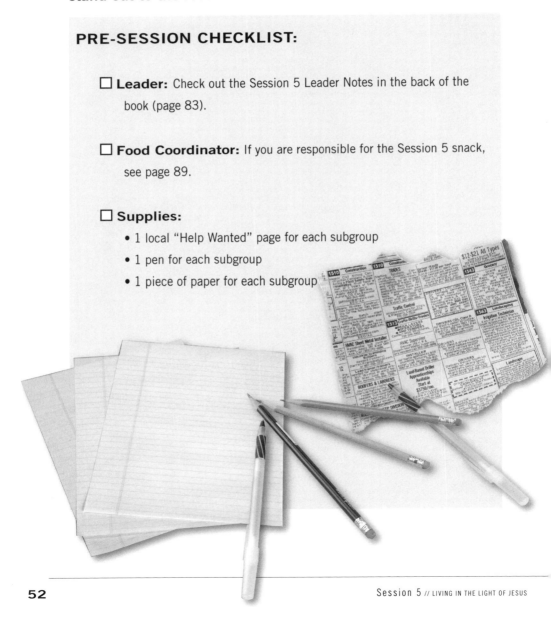

TASTE AND SEE (20 minutes)

Throughout the room are numbered bowls of chips. Grab a cup of water, find a bowl, and evaluate the chips you find there.

Take a few moments to examine each type of chip. What color, shape, and texture does it have? What does it smell like? Finally, taste a few of the chips. How does one taste different from the others? Have a sip of water to cleanse your palate; then move on to the next available bowl of chips.

After everyone's tried all of the chips, have a vote to determine the group's favorite. Then discuss the following questions:

• Which chips were the easiest to figure out?

• If this had been a blind taste test, which chips would you have been most able to distinguish? Why?

• What's one special trait or quality you believe distinguishes *you* from others?

 Watch the fifth chapter on the DVD (1 John 4:1-21).

1 John 4:1-21

[1]Dear friends, do not believe everyone who claims to speak by the Spirit. You must test them to see if the spirit they have comes from God. For there are many false prophets in the world. [2]This is how we know if they have the Spirit of God: If a person claiming to be a prophet acknowledges that Jesus Christ came in a real body, that person has the Spirit of God. [3]But if someone claims to be a prophet and does not acknowledge the truth about Jesus, that person is not from God. Such a person has the spirit of the Antichrist, which you heard is coming into the world and indeed is already here.

[4]But you belong to God, my dear children. You have already won a victory over those people, because the Spirit who lives in you is greater than the spirit who lives in the world. [5]Those people belong to this world, so they speak from the world's viewpoint, and the world listens to them. [6]But we belong to God, and those who know God listen to us. If they do not belong to God, they do not listen to us. That is how we know if someone has the Spirit of truth or the spirit of deception.

[7]Dear friends, let us continue to love one another, for love comes from God. Anyone who loves is a child of God and knows God. [8]But anyone who does not love does not know God, for God is love.

[9]God showed how much he loved us by sending his one and only Son into the world so that we might have eternal life through him. [10]This is real love—not that we loved God, but that he loved us and sent his Son as a sacrifice to take away our sins.

11Dear friends, since God loved us that much, we surely ought to love each other. 12No one has ever seen God. But if we love each other, God lives in us, and his love is brought to full expression in us.

13And God has given us his Spirit as proof that we live in him and he in us. 14Furthermore, we have seen with our own eyes and now testify that the Father sent his Son to be the Savior of the world. 15All who confess that Jesus is the Son of God have God living in them, and they live in God. 16We know how much God loves us, and we have put our trust in his love.

God is love, and all who live in love live in God, and God lives in them. 17And as we live in God, our love grows more perfect. So we will not be afraid on the day of judgment, but we can face him with confidence because we live like Jesus here in this world.

18Such love has no fear, because perfect love expels all fear. If we are afraid, it is for fear of punishment, and this shows that we have not fully experienced his perfect love. 19We love each other because he loved us first.

20If someone says, "I love God," but hates a Christian brother or sister, that person is a liar; for if we don't love people we can see, how can we love God, whom we cannot see? 21And he has given us this command: Those who love God must also love their Christian brothers and sisters.

A SENSE OF HISTORY
Distorted Ideas vs. Distinctive Truth

The infiltration of Gnostic teaching among early Christians created confusion about Jesus himself. If the physical world was bad (as Gnosticism taught), how could Jesus—who was perfectly good—have had an earthly, physical body?

This led to Docetism, an early form of Gnosticism, which taught that Jesus only *appeared* to have a physical shape but did not have an actual physical body. John refutes that belief in this chapter: "This is how we know if they have the Spirit of God: If a person claiming to be a prophet acknowledges that Jesus Christ *came in a real body,* that person has the Spirit of God" (verse 2, emphasis added).

The belief that Jesus is both fully human and fully divine has always been essential to Christian doctrine. If Jesus was not physically human (as Docetism taught), his sacrifice on the cross would have been a fraud.

John's warnings against false teachers echo other warnings throughout the New Testament (Matthew 7:15; 24:11-24; 2 Corinthians 11:13; Galatians 2:4; and 1 Timothy 1:3; 6:3).

Distortions of the truth were common in the early church, just as claims about Jesus—who he really was, what his purpose was, what he actually said, if he even *existed*—abound in today's society. From John, we learn what it means to live as a Christian in a world full of deception and what it means to shine as a bright light of truth in a dark world.

DIGGING INTO SCRIPTURE (30 minutes)

As a group, discuss:

• What thoughts or emotions came to your mind while watching this session's Bible passage?

Now break into subgroups.

Leader: Give a "Help Wanted" page to each subgroup.
Subgroup Leaders: Use a maximum of 20 minutes for your discussion time.

Take a minute to look through the Help Wanted ads together; then discuss the following:

• What are some of the more interesting jobs listed here?

• Do you meet the qualifications for any of these jobs? Which ones?

Read 1 John 4:1-21, and answer the following questions:
• What distinguishing characteristics of a Christian does John focus on in this chapter?

> *Did you know? One of the most important jobs in the world—the president of the United States—has only two job qualifications. The president must be at least 35 years old and must have been born in the United States. No other experience necessary!*

• Some people frown upon judging or critiquing others' beliefs. Yet in verses 1-6, John seems to view this as essential. Why do you (or don't you) think it's important for Christians to evaluate other beliefs and worldviews?

• Is it possible to do this without offending others? Why or why not?

• Why would loving others be such an essential part of the "testing" John tells us to do here?

Check it out! In The Message, *Eugene Peterson paraphrases 1 John 4:1 this way:* "My dear friends, don't believe everything you hear. Carefully weigh and examine what people tell you. Not everyone who talks about God comes from God. There are a lot of lying preachers loose in the world."

Leader: Give each subgroup a piece of paper and a pen or pencil.

Once you're done with your discussion, designate a writer for your subgroup. Compose your own brief "want ad," listing the qualifying traits of a true Christian based on what you've read in this chapter.

When you're done writing, come back together as a larger group. Read your "want ad" to the rest of the group; then share any other highlights or questions from your subgroup discussion.

MAKING IT PERSONAL (15 minutes)

- Read Jesus' prayer for his disciples—including John, who recorded this prayer—in the margin. How can we bring Jesus' love to the rest of the world without becoming "of the world"?

> "*I'm not asking you to take them out of the world, but to keep them safe from the evil one. They do not belong to this world any more than I do.*"
>
> —John 17:15-16

- Think back to the want ad your subgroup wrote. How can living out its "qualifications" help others discover faith in Christ? What are some real-life examples you've seen of this?

- Which qualification do you most need to develop? What's one thing you can do to begin growing in that area?

TOUCHING YOUR WORLD (25 minutes)

Review the following weekly challenge options, and select the challenge you'd like to do. Turn to a partner, and share your choice. Then make plans to connect with your partner sometime between now and the next session to check in and encourage one another.

☐ **PUT YOUR LOVE FOR OTHERS INTO ACTION.** If God has been prompting you to show greater love to others, tell your weekly challenge partner what you feel God wants you to do. Ask your partner to help you commit to a specific next step; then put your love into action.

☐ **EXAMINE WHAT YOUR CHURCH BELIEVES.** Understanding what you believe is as critical today as it was for early Christians. Get a copy of your church's doctrinal statement, statement of faith, or an essential Christian creed. Explore it; take notes about questions you have. Then get together with another Christian friend (or better yet, a pastor or church leader) to talk about what stood out to you most and to discuss any concerns you have.

☐ **WITH YOUR CHILDREN, DISCUSS DECEPTIVE BELIEFS** presented in TV and movies. Kids and teenagers may find it difficult to distinguish false beliefs and ideas from God's truth. Help them develop the skills they need to "test" the spirits by talking together after television shows, advertisements, and movies. Use open-ended questions to help your kids start thinking theologically (and critically) on their own.

☐ **INVITE A NON-CHRISTIAN FRIEND TO STUDY JESUS' LIFE WITH YOU.** If you have a friend who's spiritually curious (or at least open), invite him or her to read through one of the Gospels with you. Ask him or her to keep a journal to record observations and questions as they come up. Use your conversations as an opportunity to point out Jesus' claims and the teachings that make Christianity unique.

Come back together as a group. Share prayer requests, and then pray for everyone's needs. Take time to also thank God for each person in your group and how God has made each of them unique.

Also pray for God's wisdom to know how your uniqueness can be used to share God's love.

Until next time...

Date _____

Time _____

Place _____

Taking It Home:

1. Set a goal for how many times you'll either read through or watch on your DVD the Session 6 Bible passage (1 John 5:1-21). Make a point to read the "A Sense of History" feature in Session 6 (page 66) before the next session. If you haven't yet, now would be a good time to watch the entire book of 1 John in one sitting. (It takes about 17 minutes to watch the entire book.) Let your weekly challenge partner know what goals you've set, so he or she can encourage you and help hold you accountable.

2. Touch base sometime before the next session with your weekly challenge partner to compare notes on how you're both doing with the goals you've set.

3. If you have volunteered for a role or signed up to help with food or supplies for the next session, be sure to prepare for this. The Session 6 Supplies list can be found on page 62, and the Food Coordinator instructions are on page 89.

4. **I commit to touching my world this week by standing out for Jesus in the following ways:**

_____

_____

_____

SESSION 6:

CHOOSING LIFE IN JESUS

1 JOHN 5:1-21

In this session you'll reflect on what it means to choose to follow Jesus and how to encourage others to know Christ.

PRE-SESSION CHECKLIST:

☐ **Leader:** Check out the Session 6 Leader Notes in the back of the book (page 84).

☐ **Food Coordinator:** If you are responsible for the Session 6 snack, see page 89.

☐ **Supplies:**
- 1 pen or pencil for each person in the group
- 1 piece of construction paper for each person in the group
- 1 glue stick for each person in the group
- 1 large piece of poster board cut into the shape of a cross

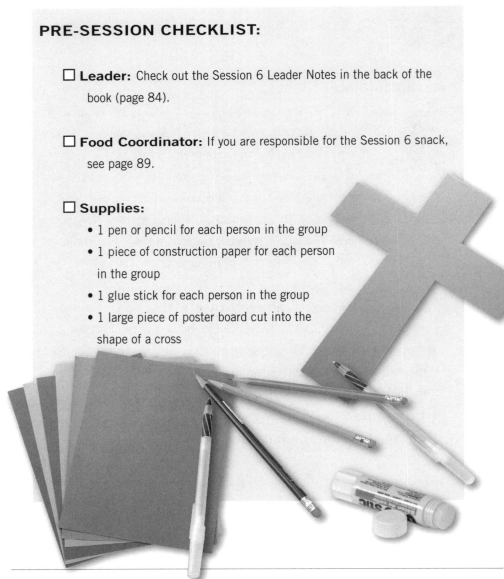

TASTE AND SEE (20 minutes)

For this session you have a choice of cookies—but just one choice. Pick one kind of cookie, and while you eat, turn to another group member and briefly share:

- What's been the best moment of your week so far?

When you're done eating and discussing, divide into two subgroups—according to the type of cookie you chose. In your subgroup, discuss the following:
- Why did you choose this kind of cookie rather than the other kind?

- Think of a time it was difficult to decide between two options—when you would have picked both if you could have. What did you finally choose, and why?

Watch the final chapter on the DVD (1 John 5:1-21).

1 John 5:1-21

¹Everyone who believes that Jesus is the Christ has become a child of God. And everyone who loves the Father loves his children, too. ²We know we love God's children if we love God and obey his commandments. ³Loving God means keeping his commandments, and his commandments are not burdensome. ⁴For every child of God defeats this evil world, and we achieve this victory through our faith. ⁵And who can win this battle against the world? Only those who believe that Jesus is the Son of God.

⁶And Jesus Christ was revealed as God's Son by his baptism in water and by shedding his blood on the cross—not by water only, but by water and blood. And the Spirit, who is truth, confirms it with his testimony. ⁷So we have these three witnesses—⁸the Spirit, the water, and the blood—and all three agree. ⁹Since we believe human testimony, surely we can believe the greater testimony that comes from God. And God has testified about his Son. ¹⁰All who believe in the Son of God know in their hearts that this testimony is true. Those who don't believe this are actually calling God a liar because they don't believe what God has testified about his Son.

¹¹And this is what God has testified: He has given us eternal life, and this life is in his Son. ¹²Whoever has the Son has life; whoever does not have God's Son does not have life.

¹³I have written this to you who believe in the name of the Son of God, so that you may know you have eternal life. ¹⁴And we are confident that he hears us whenever we ask for anything that pleases him. ¹⁵And since we know he hears us when we make our requests, we also know that he will give us what we ask for.

[16]If you see a Christian brother or sister sinning in a way that does not lead to death, you should pray, and God will give that person life. But there is a sin that leads to death, and I am not saying you should pray for those who commit it. [17]All wicked actions are sin, but not every sin leads to death.

[18]We know that God's children do not make a practice of sinning, for God's Son holds them securely, and the evil one cannot touch them. [19]We know that we are children of God and that the world around us is under the control of the evil one.

[20]And we know that the Son of God has come, and he has given us understanding so that we can know the true God. And now we live in fellowship with the true God because we live in fellowship with his Son, Jesus Christ. He is the only true God, and he is eternal life.

[21]Dear children, keep away from anything that might take God's place in your hearts.

A SENSE OF HISTORY
A Sin That Leads to Death?

John doesn't go into further explanation after mentioning "a sin that leads to death" in verse 16 of this chapter. However, this is not the only reference to a possible "unpardonable sin" in the New Testament. Many scholars believe this verse is a reference to a sin described by Jesus in Matthew 12:31-32; Mark 3:28-29; and Luke 12:10: blaspheming the Holy Spirit.

There are many different interpretations of what it means to blaspheme the Holy Spirit; the simplest, perhaps, is the idea that when a person steadfastly rejects the Holy Spirit's prompting to join God's family, that person has in essence *chosen* the consequences mentioned in verse 16.

Theologian Craig L. Blomberg puts it this way: "Probably blasphemy against the Holy Spirit is nothing more or less than the unrelenting rejection of his advances. Jesus' teaching thus parallels Acts 4:12. If one rejects the Spirit of God in Jesus, there is no one else in all the cosmos who can provide salvation."

DIGGING INTO SCRIPTURE (30 minutes)

As a group, discuss:

- What thoughts or emotions came to your mind while watching this session's Bible passage?

- What have your overall impressions been as you've interacted with the book of 1 John? How has God spoken to you through this study?

Now break into subgroups.

Subgroup Leaders: Plan to come back together in 20 minutes.

Answer the following question:

- Which word do you think better describes Christianity: *inclusive* or *exclusive*? Explain your answer.

> *"There is salvation in no one else! God has given no other name under heaven by which we must be saved."*
> —*Acts 4:12*

Turn back to page 64. Read 1 John 5:1-21. As the passage is read, underline each statement that strikes you as applying to some people while excluding others.

Answer the following questions:

- Which statements did you underline? What comes to mind as you look at these "exclusive" statements concerning your own faith and relationship with God?

> "If a man has a hundred sheep and one of them wanders away, what will he do? Won't he leave the ninety-nine others on the hills and go out to search for the one that is lost? And if he finds it, I tell you the truth, he will rejoice over it more than over the ninety-nine that didn't wander away! In the same way, it is not my heavenly Father's will that even one of these little ones should perish."
> —Matthew 18:12-14

- Now, try looking at these same statements through the eyes of a non-Christian. How would (or did) you react to these statements? What questions or feelings do these statements evoke?

- Read Matthew 18:12-14 and John 3:16, in the margin. How do these "inclusive" passages contrast with or complement the exclusive claims in 1 John 5?

> "For God loved the world so much that he gave his one and only Son, so that everyone who believes in him will not perish but have eternal life."
> —John 3:16

- Many people believe that, just like different paths all lead to the same summit of a mountain, all religions lead to heaven. Why do you think this perspective is so popular today? What do you think John's response would have been, based on this chapter?

- What are some practical ways you can respond to those who hold this perspective in a way that reflects both Jesus' love for every person and his exclusive claims as Son of God?

Come back together as a larger group, and share any highlights or questions from your subgroup discussion.

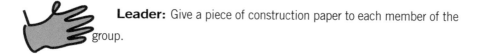 **Leader:** Give a piece of construction paper to each member of the group.

Tear your piece of construction paper into three pieces. On each piece, write one benefit of having Jesus in your life that you learned from 1 John 5 or from discoveries you've made in your own walk with Jesus.

Turn to a partner, and share what you've written. Then put all the pieces in a large pile in the center of the room.

MAKING IT PERSONAL (*??* minutes)

Take three pieces of construction paper back from the pile in the middle of the room, and break back into subgroups.

Think about three non-Christians you know—friends, family members, co-workers, or neighbors. Write the first name of each person on the blank side of that piece of paper.

Reread 1 John 5:5, 10, and 12. Then answer the following questions:

• Whose names did you write down?

> **Did you know?**
> *According to a recent Barna survey, 54 percent of American adults agree that "if a person is generally good, or does enough good things for others during their life, they will earn a place in Heaven."*

• Do the people you wrote down *really* understand what they are missing out on? Explain your answer.

• What role can you play in helping each of these people come to know Jesus and develop a relationship with him? Share ideas with one another in your subgroup.

Take time as a subgroup to pray briefly for each person written down, asking that God would use each person in the subgroup to help them discover Jesus' truth.

When you've finished praying, gather back with the larger group.

Create a colorful mosaic of your prayers. Glue your pieces of paper to the poster-board cross with the names facing *down* and the results of faith in Jesus facing outward. When all the pieces have been glued to the cross, hang it up on a wall in your meeting area.

TOUCHING YOUR WORLD (25 minutes)

Review the following weekly challenge options, and then select the challenge you'd like to do. Turn to a partner and share your choice; then make plans to connect with your partner in the next week to check in and encourage one another.

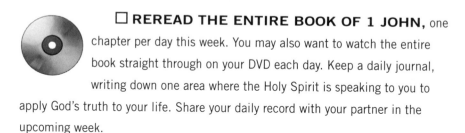 ☐ **REREAD THE ENTIRE BOOK OF 1 JOHN,** one chapter per day this week. You may also want to watch the entire book straight through on your DVD each day. Keep a daily journal, writing down one area where the Holy Spirit is speaking to you to apply God's truth to your life. Share your daily record with your partner in the upcoming week.

☐ **PRAY DAILY FOR THE THREE PEOPLE YOU WROTE DOWN.** Ask God to give you compassion and empathy for each person, as well as for boldness and wisdom to tell them about Jesus. By the end of the week, seek to have at least one spiritual conversation with at least one of these people. Invite him or her to review the exclusive claims of Jesus, and ask your friend to share his or her response. Listen openly to how your friend responds, and show respect for his or her views.

☐ **HOLD A SOCIAL EVENT AS A GROUP,** inviting non-Christian friends and family members. Plan something fun, such as a cookout, Super Bowl party, game night, or holiday celebration. As a group, commit to each invite at least one of the people represented on your mosaic prayer cross. Use this time to build meaningful relationships and show genuine love.

Come back together as a group. Share prayer requests, and then pray for everyone's needs. Also take the time to commit to follow God's leading as he uses you to draw those people represented on your mosaic to him.

Take time also to thank God specifically for things he has done in your group's lives during this study.

Leader: If you haven't already, take some time to discuss what's next for the group. Will you stay together and work on another BibleSense book? Will you celebrate your time together with a party and be done? Or will you have a party, and *then* start another BibleSense book the following week?

Touch-base time:

Set a date, time, and place to get together with your touch-base partner in the next week.

Date _____

Time _____

Place _____

Taking It Home:

1. Touch base during the week with your weekly challenge partner to compare notes on how you're both doing with the goals you've set.

2. **I commit to touching my world this week by sharing the choice of following Jesus in the following ways:**

_____

_____

_____

_____

NOTES & ROLES

CONTENTS

LEADER NOTES

General Leader Tips 75

Session 1 Leader Notes. 77

Session 2 Leader Notes. 79

Session 3 Leader Notes. 81

Session 4 Leader Notes. 82

Session 5 Leader Notes. 83

Session 6 Leader Notes. 84

GROUP ROLES

Role Descriptions 85

Group Role Tips

    Food Coordinator 88

       Food Coordinator Assignments and Ideas 88

    Host 90

    Outreach Coordinator 91

    Group Care ("Inreach") Coordinator 92

    Prayer Coordinator 93

    Subgroup Leader(s) 94

    Child Care Coordinator 95

GENERAL LEADER TIPS

1. Although these sessions are designed to require minimum advance preparation, try to read over each session ahead of time and watch the DVD chapter for that session. Highlight any questions you feel are especially important for your group to spend time on during the session.

2. Prior to the first session, watch the "Leading a BibleSense Session" overview on the DVD. You'll notice that this isn't your average Bible study. Food? Activities? Don't forget that Jesus used food and everyday items and experiences in *his* small group all the time. Jesus' disciples certainly weren't comfortable when he washed their feet (John 13:5-17) and were even a bit confused at first. Jesus reassured them, "You don't understand now what I am doing, but someday you will" (verse 7), and it turned out to be a powerful lesson that stayed with them the rest of their lives. It's our prayer that your group will have similar experiences.

3. Take the time to read the group roles on pages 85-87, and make sure all critical tasks and roles are covered for each session. The three roles you *absolutely need filled* for each session are Leader, Host, and Food Coordinator. These roles can be rotated around the group, if you like.

4. Discuss as a group how to handle child care—not only because it can be a sensitive subject but also to give your group an opportunity to begin working together *as* a group. See the Child Care Coordinator tips on page 95 for ideas on how to handle this important issue.

5. Don't be afraid to ask for volunteers. Who knows—they may want to commit to a role once they've tried it (and if it's available on a regular basis). However, give people the option of "no thanks" as well.

6. Every session will begin with a snack, so work closely with your Food Coordinator—he or she has a vital role in each session. If you need to, go ahead and ask for donations from your group for the snacks that are provided each week.

7. Always start on time. If you do this from Session 1, you'll avoid the group arriving and starting later as the study goes on.

8. Be ready and willing to pray at times other than the closing time. Start each session with prayer—let everyone know they're getting "down to business." Be open to other times when prayer is appropriate, such as when someone answers a question and ends up expressing pain or grief over a situation he or she is currently struggling with. Don't save it for the end—stop and pray right there and then. Your Prayer Coordinator can take the lead in these situations, if you like, but give him or her "permission" to do so.

9. Try not to have the first or last word on every question (or even most of them). Give everyone the opportunity to participate. At the same time, don't put anyone on the spot—remind group members that they can pass on any questions they're not comfortable answering.

10. Keep things on track. There are suggested time limits for each section. Encourage good discussion, but don't be afraid to "rope 'em back in." If you do decide to spend extra time on a question or activity, consider skipping or spending less time on a later question or activity so you can stay on schedule.

11. Don't let your group off the hook with the assignments in the "Touching Your World" section—this is when group members get to apply in a personal way what they have learned. Encourage group members to follow through on their assignments. You may even want to make it a point to ask how they did with their weekly challenges during snack time at the beginning of your next session.

12. Also note that the last weekly challenge in "Touching Your World" is often an outreach assignment that can be done either individually or as a group. Make sure that group members who take on these challenges are encouraged—and, if it's a group activity, organized. If your group has an Outreach Coordinator, let him or her take the lead here, and touch base regularly.

13. Lastly, the single most important thing a leader can do for his or her group is to spend time in prayer for group members. Why not take a minute and pray for your group right now?

Session 1 Leader Notes

1. Read the General Leader Tips starting on page 75, if you haven't already. Take a peek at the tips for other group roles as well (pages 88-95).

2. Make sure everyone has a BibleSense book and DVD. Have the group pass around their books to record contact information (page 7) before or during the "Taste and See" section, or at the end of the session.

3. If this is the first time you're meeting as a group, you may want to take a few minutes before your session to lay down some ground rules. Here are three simple ones:

- Don't say anything that will embarrass anyone or violate someone's trust.
- Likewise, anything shared in the group *stays* in the group, unless the person sharing it says otherwise.
- No one has to answer a question he or she is uncomfortable answering.

4. Take time to review the group roles on pages 85-87 before you get together, and be ready to discuss them at the end of your session. Assign as many roles as you can, but don't pressure anyone to take on something he or she doesn't want or isn't yet sure about.

5. For this session, you're responsible for the items in the Supplies list on page 8. You'll want to assign the Supplies list for future sessions; the Host is the most sensible choice to handle this responsibility, or it can be rotated around the group.

6. Unless you're ahead of the game and already have a Food Coordinator, you're responsible for the snack for this first session. You'll want to make sure you have a Food Coordinator for future sessions, but for this session, be sure to review the Food Coordinator assignment on page 88.

7. Take note of the sensory experience in "Digging Into Scripture." The Host will need to provide one room that can be darkened. Make sure there's a place for each subgroup to plug in and look at the makeup mirrors. Try to situate the mirrors so they're far enough away from each other that each subgroup is mostly in the dark, but near enough that you can find your way back to your seats as a larger group.

If you have difficulty locating a lighted makeup mirror for this activity, try this: Leave the room lights on, and use a regular mirror (a hand-held mirror is good, a tabletop mirror even better). The person looking in the mirror should position him or herself as close to the light as possible to see his or her features and "flaws" clearly.

8. Note that this experience continues and changes in "Making It Personal." Keep in mind that the group will be answering a couple of questions while the lights are off—so decide in advance how you're going to be able to *ask* those questions in the dark. Will you recite the questions from memory? Will you use a small flashlight (that lights your book but not the rest of the room)? Make sure your decision enables you to keep the rest of the group completely in the dark. Especially if this is your first time together as a group, be sensitive to people's levels of sharing during this experience—encourage but don't force. And make sure you know where the light switches are and how to get around the room in the dark!

9. Before you dismiss this first session, make a special point of reminding group members of the importance of following through on the weekly challenges each of them have committed to in the "Touching Your World" section.

10. If group members choose the "Share the light of Jesus Christ" option in "Touching Your World," arrange a time when they can compare notes and results and talk about follow-up. If you have a volunteer for Outreach Coordinator at the end of this session, this would be a great first assignment for him or her.

Session 2 Leader Notes

1. If new people join the group this session, use part of the "Taste and See" time to ask them to introduce themselves to the group, and have the group pass around their books to record contact information (page 7). Give a brief summary of the points covered in Session 1.

2. Note the Supplies list and the experience in the "Making It Personal" section. Make sure the extra chair can easily be moved to the middle of the room—a dining-room chair is ideal. Make sure everyone in your group takes a turn sitting in the chair and has the opportunity to be affirmed. If there are people who are new to the group—or if the group itself just started with Session 1—take some time before this lesson to think of creative ways to affirm people, regardless of how long you've known them. You might even take some extra time at the beginning of the session to get to know each person better so you have ideas on how to affirm them both specifically and genuinely.

It's not necessary that everyone has a comment for the person sitting in the chair, but encourage as many people as possible to share something. This can be a life-changing experience for those who have never received this kind of encouragement.

3. If you told the group you'd be following up to see how they did with their "Touching Your World" commitment, be sure to do it. This is an opportunity to establish an environment of accountability. You could use part of the "Taste and See" time to accomplish this. However, also be prepared to share how you did with your *own* commitment from the first session.

4. If group members choose the "Volunteer for an outreach ministry" option from "Touching Your World," take some time after this session to begin planning your next steps in making your participation in this event or ministry a reality. If your group has an Outreach Coordinator, talk over ideas with him or her. Also, set aside some time after your outreach to debrief the event and discover how God worked in each person's life during this time of ministry.

5. For the closing prayer time, ask for volunteers to pray for requests that were shared. If you have one, you may want to ask the Prayer Coordinator in advance to lead the prayer time. If you don't have a Prayer Coordinator, look over the Prayer Coordinator tips on page 93, and keep them in mind if you lead your prayer time. If you ask someone else to lead, try to ask in advance—and direct him or her to the Prayer Coordinator tips. Also, if your group has decided to use a prayer list, make sure you use it during your prayer time.

Session 3 Leader Notes

1. Congratulations! You're halfway through this study. It's time for a checkup: How's the group going? What's worked well so far? What might you consider changing as you approach the remaining sessions?

2. On that note, you may find it helpful to make some notes right after this session to help you evaluate how things are going. Ask yourself, "Did everyone participate?" and "Is there anyone I need to make a special effort to follow up with before the next session?"

3. Remember the importance of starting and ending on time, and remind your group of it, too, if you need to.

4. In preparation for this lesson, you might want to explore the themes of deception and false teachers more deeply. If so, look up additional passages such as Acts 20:29-30, 1 Timothy 4:1-2, and Jude 1.

5. See the Supplies list and the sensory experience in "Digging Into Scripture." You can use bandannas or scarves for blindfolds. You can even encourage group members to use their own "everyday objects" for this activity. Now here's the part we couldn't say in the session: Instruct those who aren't blindfolded to sit back down with their partners and describe the object he or she is holding in a way that would lead the blindfolded person to believe the object is something it *isn't*. For example, a CD case could be described so the blindfolded person thinks it's a cell phone ("it's flat"; "it opens up"; "it's a way of communicating"). Encourage group members to be creative in their descriptions and as convincing as they can be— even after they've given the object to their partners.

6. See also the sensory experience in "Making It Personal." You can give a sticky pad to each person, or pass a pad around and ask everyone to take three sticky notes. To make a powerful visual connection, suggest that group members place their sticky notes on their foreheads or over their hearts.

7. If there are still group roles available, discuss them with your group again. Remember, God has created each member of your group for a different purpose. As group members take on roles, they'll feel more connected to the group and will even come to feel more comfortable doing what they're not sure they want to volunteer for right now.

Session 4 Leader Notes

1. Are you praying for your group members regularly? It's the most important thing a leader can do for his or her group. Take some time now to pray for your group, if you haven't already.

2. Consider writing notes of thanks and encouragement to group members this week. Thank them for their commitment and contribution to the group, and let them know you're praying for them. (In fact, make a point of praying for them as you write their notes.) If your group has an Inreach Coordinator, encourage him or her to take on this task.

3. See the Supplies list. Note that in "Making It Personal," each group member will be taking a domino home as a reminder to live out God's love each day. Make sure you have enough expendable dominoes so group members can do this.

Session 5 Leader Notes

1. Take note of the closing question in "Taste and See." If someone in the group has difficulty seeing himself or herself as special or unique, encourage other group members to share things *they* think are special about that person. Since you did this in Session 2, it shouldn't be difficult to come up with ways this person has blessed the group—and it will serve as a powerful reminder for him or her.

2. Note the sensory experience in "Digging Into Scripture." Encourage subgroups to read quickly through the want ads so more time can be spent on the questions and the rest of the activity.

3. This would be a good time to start thinking about how you're going to celebrate finishing this study. Will you do something next week or have a party the week after? Be ready to discuss it with the group this session.

Session 6 Leader Notes

1. Since this is your group's last session from this book, make sure you have a plan for next week...and beyond.

2. What did your group decide last week? Are you having a party? Are you going directly on to another BibleSense study? Finalize your plans.

3. As part of this last session, you may want to consider having people share what this study or group has meant to them, either during the "Taste and See" section or at the end of your session. This can also be incorporated into the beginning of your prayer time if you like.

4. Take note of the Supplies list, and the sensory experience in "Digging Into Scripture" and "Making It Personal." Use a variety of colors of construction paper for this activity. Discuss with the Host in advance where you'll hang your poster-board cross.

5. Spend some extra time on the final question of this study. Help the group brainstorm a variety of ideas each person can use in sharing Jesus with their friends, relatives, and acquaintances.

6. If your group decides to coordinate a social event to invite non-Christian friends to, spend some time praying that God will lead your group through the planning process. Pray specifically that God would prepare the hearts of the people who are invited. If your group has an Outreach Coordinator, planning this event would be a perfect assignment for him or her.

7. Here's another suggestion for making the closing prayer time for this last session special: Have the group form a prayer circle. Then, if comfortable doing so, have each person or couple take a turn standing or kneeling in the middle of the circle while the group prays specifically for them. Your Prayer Coordinator is a good candidate to lead this time.

GROUP ROLES

ROLE DESCRIPTIONS

Review the group roles that follow.

We have provided multiple roles to encourage maximum participation. At minimum, there are three roles that we recommend be filled for every session— Leader, Food Coordinator, and Host. These particular roles can also be rotated around the group, if you like. Other roles (Outreach and Inreach Coordinators, especially) are best handled by one person, as they involve tasks that may take more than one week to accomplish. It's *your* group—you decide what works best. What's most important is that you work together in deciding.

Not everyone will want to take on a role, so no pressure. But as you come to own a role in your group, you'll feel more connected. You'll even become more comfortable with that role you're not so sure you want to volunteer for right now.

Read through the following roles together, and write in each volunteer's name after his or her role in your book so everyone remembers who's who (and what roles may still be available):

LEADER _____.

Your session Leader will facilitate each session, keeping discussions and activities on track. If a role hasn't yet been filled or the person who normally has a certain role misses a session, the session Leader will also make sure that all tasks and supplies are covered.

FOOD COORDINATOR _____.

The Food Coordinator will oversee the snacks for each group meeting. This role not only builds the fellowship of the group, but it is an especially important role for this particular study, since specific snacks are assigned for each session and are used to lead group members into the meaning of each session.

HOST _____.

Your Host will open up his or her home and help group members and visitors feel *at* home. It sounds simple enough, but the gift of hospitality is critical to your group. If group members don't feel welcome, chances are they won't stay group members for long. Your Host should also be responsible for supplying—or locating someone who *can* supply—the items in the Supplies list at the beginning of each session. (They're usually common household items, so don't panic.)

OUTREACH COORDINATOR _____.

Different sessions often highlight different ways to reach out—sharing the Word, extending personal invitations to others to come to your group, or participating in service projects in which your group meets the needs of those in your neighborhood or community. Your Outreach Coordinator will champion and coordinate those efforts to reach outside of your group.

GROUP CARE ("INREACH") COORDINATOR _____

_____. Everyone needs a pat on the back once in a while. Therefore, every group also needs a good Inreach Coordinator— someone who oversees caring for the personal needs of group members. That might involve coordinating meals for group members who are sick, making contact with those who have missed a session, arranging for birthday/anniversary celebrations for group members, or sending "just thinking of you" notes.

PRAYER COORDINATOR _____.

Your Prayer Coordinator will record and circulate prayer requests to the rest of the group during the week, as well as channel any urgent prayer requests to the group that may come up during the week. He or she may also be asked to lead the group in prayer at the close of a session.

SUBGROUP LEADER(S)

To maximize participation and also have enough time to work through the session, at various points we recommend breaking into smaller subgroups of three or four. Therefore, you'll also need Subgroup Leaders. This is also a great opportunity to develop leaders within the group (who could possibly lead new groups in the future).

CHILD CARE COORDINATOR _____.

Your Child Care Coordinator will make arrangements to ensure that children are cared for while their parents meet, either at the Host's house or at some other agreed-upon location(s). Depending on the makeup of your group, this could be a make-or-break role in ensuring you have a healthy group.

Again, if you don't have volunteers for every role (aside from Leader, Food Coordinator, and Host), that's OK. You may need to think about it first or become more comfortable before making a commitment. What's important is that once you commit to a role, you keep that commitment. If you know you'll miss a session, give the session Leader as much advance notice as possible so your role can be covered.

Whether you volunteer for a role now or want to think things over, take time before the next session to look over the "Group Role Tips" section that begins on the following page. You'll find plenty of useful ideas that will help your group and your role in it (or the role you're considering) to be the best it can be.

GROUP ROLE TIPS

FOOD COORDINATOR

1. Sometimes your snack will be a surprise to the rest of the group. Be sure to work closely with your Host and Leader so the timing of your snacks helps each session be the best it can be.

2. You may also need to arrive a few minutes early to set up the surprise. Set up a time with the Host for your arrival before the meeting.

FOOD COORDINATOR ASSIGNMENTS AND IDEAS

Session 1

The first session's snack is freshly baked bread. How you make the bread—from a bread maker or from store-bought bread dough—isn't nearly as important as the fact that it's freshly baked and that group members are able to enjoy the *smell* of it. Provide butter, jam, and any other toppings that would go well with your bread.

Session 2

This session's snack is:

• Milk, and...

• Cookies.

The cookies should be freshly baked (the ready-to-bake kind is fine). If you can make arrangements with the Host to bake the cookies where you're meeting before the group arrives, even better. Include different varieties of cookies, and make sure there are plenty for everyone.

Session 3

This session's snack consists of:

• Crackers—have a few different kinds available

• Spread—again, have a few different kinds available; cheese spread, butter, and mustard are all good options.

• Meat—such as pepperoni or sausage

Make sure there's plenty to choose from, as group members will build at least one mini-sandwich (and probably more—this is good stuff!) using one of each of the food items you supply.

Session 4

This session's snack is bread with jam. Provide at least a couple of different types of both bread and jam. You may also want to have a toaster available in case group members prefer their bread toasted.

If you want to provide an alternate snack as well, that's OK—but don't make it available until everyone's had the "official" snack first. You want to make sure all have enjoyed their bit of "sweetness" first.

Session 5

Supply an assortment of flavored chips, and place them each in separate bowls—you can even spread them around the room if you like. Include some unusual kinds that won't be as easily identified, such as pita chips, extra-spicy chips, or vegetable or fruit chips. Number the bowls, keeping track of which number belongs with each chip. Don't let anyone know which kinds of chips are in each bowl—hide the bags, and let group members find out for themselves.

Also, have glasses of water available for group members so they can cleanse their palates between tastes.

Session 6

For this session, put out the exact number of cookies as there are people in the group. Half of the cookies should be chocolate chip; half should be of another kind. Of course, have more cookies available for the group after your initial activity, but the object here is to force group members to make an exclusive choice. (Also, unlike your cookies in Session 2, it's not necessary that they're freshly baked. But it would be a nice touch.)

Thank you for all your work in making this a successful study!

HOST

1. Before your group gets together, make sure the environment for your session is just right. Is the temperature in your home or meeting place comfortable? Is there enough lighting? Are there enough chairs for everyone? Can they be arranged in a way that everyone's included? Is your bathroom clean and "stocked"? Your home doesn't need to win any awards—just don't let anything be a distraction from your time together.

2. Once your session has started, do what you can to keep it from being interrupted. When possible, don't answer the phone. Ask people to turn off their cell phones or pagers, if necessary. If your phone number is an emergency contact for someone in the group, designate a specific person to answer the phone so your session can continue to run smoothly.

3. If you're responsible for the supplies for your study, be sure to read through the Supplies list before each session. If there's any difficulty in supplying any of the materials, let your Leader know or contact someone else in the group who you know has them. The items required for each session are usually common household items, so most weeks this will be pretty easy. Make sure everything's set up before the group arrives.

4. Be sure also to check out what the Food Coordinator's got planned each week. Sometimes the snack is a surprise, so he or she may need your help in *keeping* it a surprise from the rest of the group. Your Food Coordinator may also need to arrive a few minutes early to set up, so be sure to work out a time for his or her arrival before the meeting.

5. And, of course, make your guests feel welcome. That's your number-one priority as Host. Greet group members at the door, and make them feel at home from the moment they enter. Spend a few minutes talking with them after your session—let them know you see them as people and not just "group members." Thank them for coming as they leave.

OUTREACH COORDINATOR

1. Don't forget: New people are the lifeblood of a group. They will keep things from getting stale and will keep your group outwardly focused—as it should be. Encourage the group to invite others.

2. Don't overlook the power of a personal invitation—even to those who don't know Jesus. Invite people from work or your neighborhood to your group, and encourage other group members to do the same.

3. Take special note of the "Touching Your World" section at the end of each session. The last weekly challenge is often an outreach assignment that can be done either individually or as a group. Be sure to encourage and follow up with group members who take on these challenges.

4. If group members choose an outreach option for their weekly challenge, use part of your closing time together to ask God for help in selecting the right service opportunity and that God would bless your group's efforts. Then spend some time afterward discussing what you'll do next.

5. Consider having an event before you begin your BibleSense study (or after you finish it). Give a "no obligation" invite to Christians and non-Christians alike, just to have the opportunity to meet the others in your group. Do mention, however, what the group will be studying next so they have an opportunity to consider joining you for your next study. Speak with your Leader before making any plans, however.

6. As part of your personal prayer time, pray that God would bring new people to the group. Make this a regular part of your group's prayer time as well.

GROUP CARE ("INREACH") COORDINATOR

1. Make a point of finding out more about your group members each week. You should be doing this as a group member, but in your role as Inreach Coordinator, you'll have additional opportunities to use what you learn to better care for those in your group.

2. If a group member has special needs, be sure to contact him or her during the week. If it's something the group can help with, get permission first, and then bring the rest of the group into this ministry opportunity.

3. Find out the special dates in your group members' lives, such as birthdays or anniversaries. Make or bring cards for other group members to sign in advance.

4. If someone in your group is sick, has a baby, or faces some other kind of emergency, you may want to coordinate meals for that person with the rest of the group.

PRAYER COORDINATOR

1. Pray for your group throughout the week, and encourage group members to pray for one another. Keep a prayer list, and try to send out prayer reminders after each session.

2. Be sure to keep your group up to date on any current or earlier prayer requests. Pass on "praise reports" when you have them. Remind them that God not only hears, but *answers* prayer.

3. Remember that the role is called Prayer *Coordinator*, not "Official Pray-er for the Group" (whether that's what your group would prefer or not). At the same time, some members of your group may be uncomfortable praying aloud. If there are several people in your group who don't mind praying, one person could open your prayer time and another close it, allowing others to add prayers in between. Give everyone who wants to pray the opportunity to do so.

4. Prayers don't have to be complex, and probably shouldn't be. Jesus himself said, "When you pray, don't babble on and on as people of other religions do. They think their prayers are answered merely by repeating their words again and again" (Matthew 6:7).

5. If some group members are intimidated by prayer, begin prayer time by inviting group members to complete a sentence as he or she prays. For example, ask everyone to finish the following: "Lord, I want to thank you for..."

6. Don't overlook the power of silent prayer. Don't automatically fill "dead spaces" in your prayer time—God may be trying to do that by speaking into that silence. You might even consider closing a session with a time of silent prayer.

SUBGROUP LEADER(S)

1. These sessions are designed to require a minimum of preparation. Nonetheless, be sure to read over each session and watch the DVD in advance to get comfortable with those sections where you may be responsible for leading a subgroup discussion. Highlight any questions you think are important for your subgroup to spend time on for next session.

2. Try not to have the first or last word on every question (or even most of them). Give everyone the opportunity to participate. At the same time, don't put anyone on the spot—let subgroup members know they can pass on any question they're not comfortable answering.

3. Keep your subgroup time on track. There are suggested time limits for each section. Encourage good discussion, but don't be afraid to "rope 'em back in." If you do decide to spend extra time on a question or activity, consider skipping or spending less time on a later question or activity so you can stay on schedule.

CHILD CARE COORDINATOR

There are several ways you can approach the important issue of child care. Discuss as a group which alternative(s) you'll use:

1. The easiest approach may be for group members to each make their own child care arrangements. Some might prefer this; others may not be able to afford it on their own. If a parent or couple needs financial assistance, see if someone else in the group can help out in this area.

2. If your meeting area is conducive to it, have everyone bring their children to the meeting, and have on-site child care available so parents can pay on a child-by-child basis.

3. If most or all of your group members have young children, you could also consider rotating child care responsibilities around the group rather than paying someone else.

4. If there are members in your group with older children who are mature enough to watch the younger children, pay them to handle your child care. Maybe they can even do their own lesson. If so, Group offers a number of great materials for children of all ages—go to www.group.com to find out more.

5. Check to see if the youth group at your church would be interested in providing child care as a fundraiser.

> **Important:** It is wise to prescreen any potential child care worker—paid or volunteer—who is watching children as part of a church-sanctioned activity (including a home Bible study). Your church may already have a screening process in place that can be utilized for your group. If not, Group's Church Volunteer Central network (www.churchvolunteercentral.com) is a great resource, containing ready-made background-check and parental-consent forms as well as articles and other online resources.